To My
Pastor ymon
Thank you for
your Support!

Lillian Cunningham
2015

How to Meet and

Marry a

in a Few Easy Steps

How? You Do It God's Way!

LILLIAN P. CUNNINGHAM

WESTBOW
P R E S S®
A DIVISION OF THOMAS NELSON
& ZONDERVAN

Scripture taken from the King James Version of the Bible.

WestBow Press books may be ordered through booksellers or by contacting:

WestBow Press
A Division of Thomas Nelson & Zondervan
1663 Liberty Drive
Bloomington, IN 47403
www.westbowpress.com
1 (866) 928-1240

ISBN: 978-1-4908-8452-3 (sc)

Library of Congress Control Number: 2015909593

Print information available on the last page.

WestBow Press rev. date: 07/16/2015

Inspirations And Dedications

Giving Thanks to God in all his Glory, to Jesus Christ our Lord and Savior, and to the Holy Spirit that gave the inspiration to write this short book. I also want to acknowledge my family, loving husband and Pastor, Reverend William A. Cunningham, my beautiful daughter Danielle LaShawn Gray, my only grandson, William O'Shea Gray Jr, and my big sister Gracie M. Johnson. To all my nieces and nephews here in Detroit, Michigan, To my Auntie Clara Shipp, and to all my *crazy cousins* in Illinois and Texas, I want to thank you all for the love you have shown me over the years, I love you too. Thanks for being *My Family*.

Last but not least, I want to thank my church family, the members of the World Wide Missionary Baptist Church of Detroit, Michigan. A church that is known as: *The Friendly Church,* a place where all visitors are welcomed with open arms. It is a *Spiritually, centered* church filled with members who love the Lord. Committed Saints of Jesus Christ, loving people who come to church to give God all Praise and Honor, and to worship *Him in Spirit and in Truth.*

Of course there are some, as we know it, who come on Sunday for different reasons. Some, only to see what the Pastor's wife is wearing that day, or to hear certain choir members sing, or to go to sleep during the worship service. I ask that you please wake up, pay attention, and take notice as the preached word is going forth. And to those folks who are getting caught up in the *Emotional* but not the

Spiritual Praise of the worship service, I say to you, come on people, and let us praise God for *real* on this Christian journey!

During the worship service we need to be awake and alert, when the Word of God is being preached. This may be the day that God sends your blessing through a message to us by the minister. However, some us prefer to sleep when *God's Word* is going forth and we miss our blessing! Wake up! Pay Attention! Stop Playing, and be genuine in your Christian walk. (Life) And to my husband's good friend Reverend Jake Gaines, I want to Thank you for your guidance and for your assistance to such a *New Writer* as *Myself,* your advice was important to me and much appreciated in the writing of this little book. Finally to the non-well-wishers, this book is dedicated to you too!

Thank You, and Bless The Lord!

This is a book of Christian Beliefs, referencing various scriptures from the Holy Bible that pertain to our daily living. The Bible is the True Believers guideline for life.

What is a True Believer? Well, let me explain:

The True Believer is of the Christian faith, one who totally believes that our Heavenly Father, God, sent his son, Jesus, to earth to be the ultimate sacrifice to save mankind from their sins. St. John 3:16 (King James Version Bible)

The True Believer: One who has given his or her life to Christ, one who has repented, and has been forgiven of their sins by confessing to Christ Jesus.

True Believers, believe in the Gospel of Jesus Christ, and totally believe as well as trusts that God is the Sovereign King and Ruler of their lives.

The True Believers have committed their lives to being missionaries and witnesses to spread the Gospel of Jesus Christ to all mankind. They believe the bible is true and that when we die, the physical body is buried in the ground, returning to dust, but our spiritual body or our soul lives and will be present with God in heaven. II Corinthians 5:6-8

The Christian believes that Jesus is coming back again to take us home to live in heaven with God. The True Believer believes that if we live right and are obedient to the Will of God, according to God's Holy Scriptures, we will live eternally with Him in Heaven. This defines the term True Believers. We as Christians believe in the Gospel, What is the Gospel? It is the biblical truth that Jesus came, lived, died, and rose on the third day with All Power in heaven and in earth. These Divine acts of Christ are also known as the Good News Story. Christians believe that a *resurrected Jesus* rose from the grave, and ascended back to heaven to sit at the right hand of his father, *God.* However, Jesus didn't leave us alone on earth. He left us the *Holy Ghost (The third part of the Holy Trinity.)*

(Note: the Holy Trinity is defined as: God the Father (Creator) Jesus, Gods only son, (The Savior of the world) and the Holy Ghost. (The Spiritual Comforter) This definition is biblically known as the Trinity or the Godhead.

The Holy Ghost/Comforter came to mankind after Jesus ascension back to heaven. Jesus told the disciples that he would not leave the Christian Believers *Comfortless.* (Alone). *St. John 14:18*

Since the resurrection from the grave and the ascension of Jesus to heaven, the promise to mankind from Jesus has been kept, that he wouldn't leave us alone, and that He would come again to man to take us home to live in heaven with Him. God's promise to return. This is called the _Rapture._ *John 14: 1-4, Acts 1:1, Revelations 1:7*

Thousands of years have passed since the acts of the cross, and the world has changed over the generations, but God's Power and his Love for mankind has remained the same. *Hebrews 13:5*

Christians believe that every word of the Bible is true. Christians also believe that God is Omnipresent, (everywhere at the same time) Omniscient (sees and knows everything in the entire world) and Omnipotent. (all powerful) Christians also believe that the Holy Spirit dwells within our repented hearts.

The Comforter is the Spiritual gift and guide from God that lives in the heart of every Christian believer.

This is what the Christians or the True Believers have pledged their lives to, the perfect Gospel of Jesus Christ. As mentioned before, we believe the Bible to be true in its entirety.

The Bible is simply defined as: *the Believer's Instructions Before Leaving Earth. B.I.B.L.E.* A very bright teen in our Youth Sunday School informed of us this quote from a previous bible class he had attended at another church.

The Bible is God's Living Word! Did you hear me? It bears repeating. The Bible *is* God's Living Word. God said it, and I believe it!

If you do not believe in God today, and want to turn your life around then you need to read the Bible and this book. Then, ask God to make a change in your life. All can be saved who believe in Him. *Romans 10: 8, 9, thru 13*

Of course, if you are a hard-core atheist, refusing to believe that there is a God, or you are refusing to believe that there is a Heaven or a Hell. If you are determined to be a nonbeliever all of your life, then this book and the Bible are NOT for you. You, the non-believer, have your mind made up. You, the non-believer, are blind to the Gospel Truth, and you have an *I can't see God, so he doesn't exist attitude.*

Therefore, the only logical thing for you to do is to deny the *existence* of God. In the bible the non-believers are referred to as *fools. Psalms 14:1*

It is not our job as Christian Missionaries to beg you to come to Christ. But we will continue to pray for you that you may one day *see God as we see Him, and come to love God, as we love Him.* After that, it's up to God to make the change in you. We are simply Missionaries that go out into the world to *Proclaim Jesus* to you. If you don't want to hear it, God says to move on to someone else who will listen. *Matthew 10: 14* It is not our job as believers to argue God's Word with you nor to prove or show you God through debate! The Bible is our reference. We speak on the word of God, not on our opinion of what the scripture is saying. God inspires the bible scriptures in its entirety. *II Timothy 3: 16*

The believer most certainly can elaborate on the biblical scriptures as the Holy Spirit aides him or her in explaining it to the nonbeliever, but the believers can only use their own testimony of how good God is to them as an example when witnessing to the nonbelievers.

The believer must refer to the Bible regarding the existence of God as the Holy Spirit gives it to him or her to aid in *witnessing* to the nonbeliever.

The believer can boldly proclaim the saving goodness of Jesus, but only the Father in heaven can draw them in through the teachings of Jesus Christ.

St. John 6:44

So, come on people! Let's go on a journey to see how to live our lives God's Way!

Table of Contents

He Who Finds...

The Bible states in *Proverbs 18:22 King James Version:* "*Whoso (who so ever) finds a wife finds a good thing, and obtains favor of the Lord.*"

He who finds a wife ... finds a good thing. *He*, who finds a wife ...First of all, the verse indicates finding someone, a *wife*, not a *girlfriend* to live with, but a *wife,* to share your life with. God *honors* marriage. *Hebrews 13:4*

The Bible is talking about finding and marrying someone who possesses moral character, someone who is true to you and honest in behavior.

A man should be seeking someone who would be proud to be his wife, And to be the mother of his children. The man should be seeking a woman who possesses *Spiritual and Moral* standards. Unfortunately for some men, a Good Woman really *is* hard to find. For others, their prayers were answered right off, and they found the woman of their dreams, and they have been married for what seems like forever.

There are many good men looking for good women, but they're falling short. Don't you know that God wants everyone to have a husband or a wife? *No man is an island, no man stands alone.*

This quote is not a bible verse, but it's a good quote nonetheless. God does not want us to be alone. He honors marriage!

God has these blessings set up for you, but some of us don't want the blessings, because we don't want to do it *God's Way* in order to get that good spouse. We think we can do it on our own. Not!

I've stated a truth: a good woman *is* hard to find. Why? Because we are giving men our bodies sexually on the first date!

We've got him in the bedroom before the date is over and before his dinner can digest properly, we're trying to sexually capture our date into an early commitment of marriage! We have to stop being so anxious ladies. Take your time. If possible, build a relationship with each other. Date for a while; learn everything you can about each other. And ask God if this is the one for you. Give your love a chance to grow and to bloom. In the beginning of the relationship, talk to each other.

Have an intelligent conversation with him. You can find out a lot just by talking to the man. If you can engage him in simple small talk, and he is vibrant in making complete and intelligent sentences, he may be worth a second date. However, if you notice on that first date, his whole conversation is *"Yo, You Know What I mean"*, *"What it is Baby?"* *"Looka here,"* *"Uh, Duh,"* *"I don't have No Job yet, but I got some stuff in the works, I been working on it since I was 18."* Yeah, *I know I'm thirty years old, but these "thangs" take time Boo!"*

And my personal favorite quote of all time from a man is: *"Where do I live?"* *"Well, I live at my Mamma's house for now, till this "thang" I got going takes off."* Really? You ask yourself, is he joking? Quit playing! He can't be serious you should be saying to yourself! If you are met with this type of man, I say to you, it's time to end the Carnival Show! Girl, the date is OVER! Excuse yourself, Get up, and Get out!

Leave him right there! Run. Don't walk to the nearest exit! After a while when he realizes that you're gone, he'll call his boys, Pookie and Ray-Ray, to come and pick him up. In the words of that famous R & B singer, Ms. Erica Badue: *"You" (meaning He) better call "Tyrone!"*

Here's another thing we women must stop doing:

Don't invite every new man you meet to your house. You don't know enough about him. He may be the son of Satan, just Evil. This new guy you've just met could be like a roach, he got in easily, he likes his new surroundings, and now you can't get rid of him, no matter how much Bug Spray and Smoke Bombs you put out! Single women don't move your boyfriend into your house! Don't pretend to be married by living *Common Law*. But get married for real in the sight of God!

I'm just saying …

Do Not Be Intimidated By...
Or Appear Weak To A Man!

Now, don't get mad at me if you're that woman. Don't get mad at me if you're sleeping with every Tom, Dick, and Jamaal in the city. It is your fault if you are getting pregnant by all your babies daddies. And they leave you for another weak woman like yourself. Take it from me you cannot hold a man with just sex, no matter who you are. I know I tried it in my young life. Surprised? Honey, I'm being for real in this book. I'm not going to *sugar coat* it. I'm not going to tell you that it was all roses and springtime growing up as a teen to young womanhood and that I didn't do anything wrong. Baby, I messed up just like some of you. But Praise Be to God I got up out of that mud puddle, and went running to God for help. So much for me however, I'm married now and living happily with Reverend Cunningham. We are talking about single, beautiful, intelligent women like yourselves, who feel you have to use your body to get what you want. No, darling, you don't.

You have to be a strong woman who doesn't give in to a man's charms and persuasiveness so easily. Ok, so you say to yourself, I am a *strong woman*, and I know how to handle myself. I am *Not*, intimidated by any man! *He*, better be intimidated by me! *I am not easily sucked in by the Male Player Games* You say to yourself. *I'm a strong woman! I have a college degree! I own my own business, I am successful, and I'm financially set! I've got it all together! What man can break me down? The thought of my being weak is preposterous, you vainly mumble under your breath!* Then the weirdest thing happens … changing everything.

<u>*Note: Defining Male Player Games:*</u>

These are Strategies that men use to entice, capture, and allure women like hunters perusing their prey. He physically, intimately, and emotionally toys with the female for a time during the dating game, offering hollow promises of them being together forever, but never committing to a relationship as a couple. He breaks down every defense barrier she puts up until she gives in to his pursuit by waving the white flag, throwing in the towel, and proclaiming that he is the love of her life. Now, he is living in your house, not working, driving your car, and waving at you from the front window as you go off to work to support him! Something is very wrong with these pictures, ladies! Once the *hunter has captured his game, by using his alluring charms, his strong persuasions, and his good looks, he soon gets bored with her, for the challenge of pursuit has grown cold, and the chase to conquer is not as exciting anymore with his present mate. So, he quickly moves on to his next challenging pursuit with another innocent woman. And so on, and so on, as he uses one unsuspecting female after another through the years.*

Not caring about any of the women he has wronged nor does he care about all the hurt he has caused them. He has used these women for his own selfish games of getting into the female's life, scoring sexually, and adding another female conquest to his belt notch, with no committed strings of marriage. And then he moves on to the next female target as quickly as possible. This is Male Player Games defined by my husband William Cunningham, from a male perspective, and from my living this life as a very young, naive female.

Moving On ... A Case Scenario

You're out one day shopping, running a few errands, just minding your own business, just doing *you*. You're tired and hungry from shopping all day and you stop at the local café, for a quick bite to eat and to relax for a few minutes. The place is not that busy, but it's busy enough where you have to sit at the back booth by the window.

There is an empty table right at the window, and you think *Maybe I should sit there*. Changing your mind, you say to yourself, *No, too much sun*. So you sit down at the booth with your sandwich and drink facing the window, just looking out at the busy streets watching the people pass by, eating your lunch and minding your own business. When, all of a sudden this nice smelling man sits down at the window table in front of you. (The sent of his cologne already made you look towards him when he walked by your table.) He smelled so good; the aroma caught your nose forcing you to look away from the window and the activity outside. His cologne tantalized your nostrils, as it captured your attention to want to see the face of the man that smelled so good. Still enjoying *his* aroma in the air, you also took notice of the man's *physic* in those straight legged, boot cut blue jeans he was wearing.

Nice, you're thinking as you quickly glanced at him passing by you. As you continue sneaking quick peeks at *Mr. Fine,* you also noticed that he couldn't decide which way he wanted to sit at his table. First, he was sitting at the table with his back to you, but he turned around, away from the sunny window, and now he is sitting with his back to the window, facing you from the next table! Oh my! He is so cute, you say to yourself as you try not to stare. He catches your glance, and he smiles at you. You smile back at him, quickly looking down at your sandwich, while thinking, *God Bless his mother and father*! They did a great job! You wonder, *now, why is my heart pounding so fast?* Strange. But wait, pause break here, for a question? Is this the strong, *independent woman* going weak in the knees for the very cute man? Is this *you*, who said you wouldn't fall for any of the *male player games?* All he did was smile at you, *Miss Independent, Miss College Degree,* and instantly you have forgotten all that you said you *wouldn't do.* In your mind, you have already pictured a June wedding to this man at the next table. What happened? Let's face it, ladies; we can get weak when it comes to the opposite sex. Sometimes we forget we have a brain.

But we must compose ourselves and be strong. Don't let him see any desperation on your part. Don't let him see you sweat. Be cool, and by all means, remain a *Lady!*

Then, out of the blue, the cute man asks to join you at your table. You smile and nod yes. As he gathers his food and begins to walk over, you give yourself the speech: *Be calm girl. Remember you are an intellectual! But Oh My! He is Fine to the one-hundredth degree!*

As he approaches, you're checking out his body and that alluring walk of his, and all the while your mind is screaming, *Honey, I will marry you today and have your babies, all five of them!* I say to you, hold on and come back to reality Miss College! Not yet! At least find out what his name is. You wonder, why is everything in slow motion? Hopefully you are not saying what you are thinking out loud, but your thoughts are blaring in your ears. Please, don't let me say something stupid! As he reaches your table, you get a closer view of him. Your body is having an inside party, complete with fireworks, while on the outside you are trying very hard to keep your composure.

7

You smile weakly, and for some reason sweat gathers around the top of your lips and on your forehead! Then, you start to giggle like you're five years old. What's that all about? You say to yourself. Man, this was the longest walk ever from this big body of fineness to my table. I'm in Love! Marry Me! You scream silently in your head! Is this man real, or did they put something in my drink? While he was coming over you were thinking, he looks so good, your nose caught a whiff of his cologne again, he smells wonderful, you said to yourself. The aroma of *Gucci For Men* had gotten to the table before he did!

That tight shirt he's wearing is screaming against those bulging muscles, his face is a work of art; so gentle looking, yet his features are strong and masculine. And those attractive lips, with those even white teeth peering through those luscious lips, showing that infectious smile, perfection!

Did I see dimples? I've got to be dreaming, he's not real! You're thinking. Then as he stands before you at your table with his tray in hand, speaking to you, you can't understand a word he said. Funny, in your dazed state of mind, you see his lips move, but you can't hear what he's saying for some reason. I'm sorry, what did you say? You ask him. He repeats his name. Oh, he said his name is Trevor, Hi Trevor, nice to meet you as you gesture for him to sit down. Trevor says it's nice to meet you too. Then Trevor asks, what's your name? You know mine, so what's yours? You began to tell him, but you stop, suddenly you have developed *brain freeze*, and you can't think of your own name! My name is … *Oh my! You think in horror, what's my name? It's…I can't think! Help me! I know I've got one, what is my name? I'm so overwhelmed by this man; I have forgotten! Now he's looking at me like I'm crazy! You're thinking,* as you look into his face, with a confused look on yours.

*Helpful advice: Here's where you calm down, take a deep breath, gather yourself, and draw **you** back to earth. Once you have calmed down, and regrouped, once the blood has finally come back to your brain, and your memory bank is functioning again, you will start to remember those important things, like your name for instance!*

The Conversation

So, now begins the conversation. It's good to have a nice conversation in the beginning. There is a world of topics you can talk about. You don't know what the two of you have in common yet, until you sit down and have a conversation together. I know it seems crazy, but, during that moment, within your heart and mind, you need to ask the Lord to give you strength, to make the *right choices* concerning your new friendship. And he will. Of course, you want this nice looking person to be more to you than just a friend, because you have higher aspirations for the two of you. Such as, *Love, Commitment, and Marriage!* But the key is, *He has to want you too.* Let him get to know you, give him a chance to learn what your likes and dislikes are, if possible, develop a relationship with each other over time. Pray and ask God if this is the one for you. It doesn't hurt to ask God to guide you to your perfect mate. Become friends before you become a married couple. A healthy friendship can sometimes turn into love, which can lead to marriage. But, the man has to *want and desire you* so much, until he falls in *love* with you, he *can't live without you,* and *he feels his life is incomplete,* until *the two of you marry.*

Ladies you cannot get that type of *want from a midnight or morning booty call, you* cannot obtain a productive, loving, relationship, if the man doesn't respect you, or see you as the beautiful woman that you are. *That horrible B-word name* that women are called is not your name! Respect yourself! You have a name and you should be called by it. Remember this: You don't have to take insults from any man, just to say you have a man. Love does not destroy or tear down. First learn to love yourself.

I'm Beautiful!

Beautiful, that's what you are. We are all beautiful in Gods sight, because we were fashioned by God. And honey, God doesn't make junk! So ladies learn to love yourselves, take a good look in the mirror at yourself and see your beauty from top to bottom. See how your eyes are clear and gleaming, holding the mysteries to your soul. God made us special. Every part of your body is beautiful, even your hair. Seriously, ladies we possess glorious hair, in long or short styles. Yes ladies our hair is an attraction to men, for some reason they just have to touch it. A man would want to gather our hair in his hands to smell the sweet fragrance of it but, Umm...No...Wait, Time Out! On second thought, Don't Touch The Hair! The worst thing a man could do is mess up a Sisters Hair! As for those *Other Sisters* with that hair that falls back in place, he can touch *your* hair! But, to the ones like me, who are trying to make their hairdo last until they go to the beauty shop next week, Hands off Man! Don't touch the glorious hair!

Well, anyway as I have said, big or small, short or tall, long hair, short hair, or no hair, we are all precious in God's sight! Praise God! Ladies help our single men find a good wife, by being an upright lady. *Psalms 15:2,* and also while we are trying to live *upright*, we also want to obtain *Favor, Grace, Mercy, and Blessings of the Lord.*

Believe in yourself ladies, lift your head up and be proud. If you see yourself as nothing, others will see you as nothing also. Be positive about yourself and trust God's teachings. Quote this bible verse: *I can do all things through Christ that strengthens me.*

Philippians 4:13

Think about it, ladies you've tried it your way, and it hasn't worked out. Why not try it God's way?

Make Some Changes

If you want to find a good husband, there are some changes you have to make in your life. You cannot live in the past, thinking about what happened thirty years ago when you *were* happy. I'm not going to believe you haven't been happy for thirty years, even five years ago. Why did you stay in the rut so long? Girl, get up and start living your life! As we continue to talk about making those life changes, the first change, is to *make God The Head of your life, period*. That means *He comes first*, before you, before your family, before your job, before your money, before your parents. I don't care how much you love Mama and Papa. God must be *first* in your life. Seek God first! *Matthew 6:33*

Long Term Unhappiness

Have you ever wondered why your life seems to be the same year after year? Have you wondered why the *True Believers* are achieving their goals, moving forward, and being blessed more than you? I know some of you have asked yourself these questions: Why not me Lord? Why can't I get some blessings? I go to church! Why don't I have a man? Well, step back and look at the situation. Maybe you haven't made *God the Center* of your life, but the *True Believers* have. Maybe some of you are still *playing church*, but the *True Believers* are true in their faith. They have a Spiritual Relationship and Connection to God and the Holy Spirit dwells within them. Maybe you just come to church, as a formality, or a tradition, and sadly, you leave church as empty as when you came.

On the other hand, the *True Believers* soak up God's word, then, they applied it to their lives. They have committed themselves to strive to be better people before God and Society. Why? Could it be some of us came to church just as the *True Believers* do, but hear *none* of the preached word? Maybe they sit in a daze for an hour and a half during the *Worship Service,* only becoming alert when it was time for the *Benediction* to end the service. And what about you paying your *Tithes and Offerings?* Ask yourself could it be we don't trust God enough to pay our *Tithes* or to give *a Financial Offering?* Could it be because of our lack of trust in being obedient to God, we give God what we think *He* should have instead of what *God commands us to do as stated in His word?* With this way of thinking, we take on a different character. We become *robbers and thieves. Malachi 3:8-10.* The *True Believers* are *obedient* to the Word. They give a tenth of their earnings, or a tenth of their time to God *cheerfully.* This point aggravates some of you. You ask why should *I* give God *my* money? First of all it's not *your* money. Everything belongs to *God! Psalms 24:1 You* Own *Nothing!*

You wonder why you can't make ends meet, even though you work all week and do overtime. It seems as if you have holes in your pockets, and you can't figure out where your money is going. The answer is: you have not given God what he has commanded you to give. *Malachi 3:8-10. Are we aware that we are robbing God?*

And to those of you who have all the money, all of the education, and you have every material possession that you've ever wanted, if you do not have Jesus in your life then you are as empty, and lifeless as your possessions. *I John 5:12*

It's true, education and having money are important, still, we need God in our lives. Don't let *Material* possessions outweigh and bog down your *Spiritual* possessions to live for Christ. *Hebrews 12:1-2*

No, God does not need *your* money. It's *His* anyway. God continues to reveal to us in his holy word that we must love *Him* more than the mighty dollar. *I Timothy 6:10, 11*

Giving is also a part of the Christian's requirements. *II Corinthians 9:6, 7*

It's a simple process that God has put before us. We just need to follow it. I know some of you are saying you're as successful as ever and you don't go to church, and you don't believe in any god! And I say to you that *YOU* are only enjoying the *Blessing of the Saints of God!* The true believers are the ones who prayed for this world, the ones who continue to pray diligently for all people in this world, for people that they know and don't know. They pray continually for their families, for their community, and for their own strength to continue on this Christian walk. They are *obedient to the Will of*

God and strive daily to walk in Gods righteousness. The non-believers are receiving broken chunks from the Believer's Blessings! You don't believe it. Look it up, *Matthew 5:45*

Let it be known today *that everything belongs to God* and it is by *Gods Will* that you have what you have. *Psalms 24:1-6*

When Praises Go Up!

Prayer and Praise, they go hand in hand. God listens to hear our prayers, and he answers them. Sometimes what may not seem like an answer really *is* an answer. Even if our answer from God is no, or wait, it's an answer. Unfortunately some of us don't know how to pray, or bother to pray at all. Here is a starter prayer, I would like to suggest for you in *Matthew 6: 9-13*

Get your bible out and read. It's always good to search the scriptures and read bible passages for yourself.

It's important that we realize that *prayer* is the communication line to heaven. It is our private talk between God and us, here's where we ask an all-knowing God for what ever we are standing in need of. *Matthew 7:7*

Praise is the undying love and reverence of our Lord. We praise God, not just for what he can do, or what he has done in our lives. We Praise and Honor God for Who He is: our Creator, our Lord and Savior, our Safety Zone, God is our Everything. Bless the Lord! As Christian women we should embrace and trust God for his Greatness, His Kingship, His Great Power, and His Love and Mercy for us. No one else came and endured the torture of the cross for a wretch like us. St. John 19:17-37, Mark 15:21-37

And after reading these verses, you too can proclaim, *what love the Father has for me!*

Please read *St. John 3:16* it confirms Gods love for us. That's why we must continue to Praise and Glorify His Holy Name. Not just on Sunday, but everyday of our lives! Bless the Lord!

Be Grateful and Say Thank You

We should also be *Thankful.* Our prayers, our praise, even our songs should reflect our *Gratefulness.* When God touches you with a finger of love and wakes you up in the morning, you should say *Thank You Lord, for one more day. He* didn't have to wake you, but *He* did because *He* loves you. God owes us *nothing.* We owe *Him everything.* Give God praise even when you are having a *funky day.* Don't give into the evils of Satan and self-pity. Never believe that you have a problem that can't be solved. *God can do all things, and nothing is impossible for God. St. Luke 1:37*

Learn to praise God in the midst of the *storm,* learn to praise God in your *midnights,* even in your *contentions Psalms 46:1. Pray and Praise your way out* of a situation. God will *deliver* you to *peace.* Give God the praises of which he so deserves. *Praise His Holy Name!*

A New Mind

If you want change in your life, you have to get up and make a change. Renew your mind; forget about the old you. And start to focus on finding the *new* you. *Romans 12:2*

Ladies, start transforming yourself into a better you! I like that old cartoon show called the Transformers. It was really cool the way the transformers would look like plain everyday cars and trucks on the road, but when trouble came upon them or threatened humanity, these plain everyday vehicles detected danger and began to change their outward appearance from mild-mannered to *Fighting Warriors* by standing up and being *Transformed* into special battle weapons to fight off the evildoers. That's how we as Christians should be, even when there's peace in the land we should be laying low, living our ordinary lives, but dressed for battle in the whole armor of God, always watching. Then when trouble comes, *we should be standing up, girded up, prayed up, armored up, and ready to fight. Ephesians 6:10-18*

What Are You Praying for?

OK, this last point will really throw you for a loop. Stop praying all day, 24/7, for God to send you a man! God is not stupid, He is not forgetful, and He is not deaf. He heard your prayers when you prayed it the first time, three years ago! He knows what you need and he will give it to you WHEN HE IS READY! Again, *he said it in his Word that he would give you the desires of your heart. Psalms 37:4 However* God is not moving fast enough for you right? So you go out ahead of Him and marry the first man that comes along, not knowing anything about his character. Quickly marrying someone who you have nothing in common with, you are two strangers uniting in Holy Matrimony. Bad mistake.

You started fishing around in the waters of life for a man, but you were fishing in shallow waters, close to the shore, catching weak, dead fish, tin cans, mud, and lots of garbage. So here you are today trying to maintain a relationship with someone you don't even want, just to say you have a man. Had you waited on God, he would have told you to cast your net into the deep where the *good fish* (men) are. But, you couldn't wait. Now you're praying to God to help you get out of this terrible relationship, and you've got the nerve to be upset because God isn't moving fast enough for you? Honey, God is not on your time. In fact he is above time. *Revelation 1:8*

We live by a clock, but God doesn't. Still we want God to hurry up and bless us, regardless. We want all God's blessings in spite of our sinful lifestyle.

Now, think about it. Why would God send you a good man, when your lifestyle is so messed up? Why would God give you a good man when your temple (you) is raggedy and sinful? Why would God give you a good man when you are so disobedient and so dysfunctional? How can God talk to you when you are so high on drugs, so plastered on alcohol, or so promiscuous? Why would God send you anything good? Ouch! Is this description you? Did it hit a nerve? Sorry, but right is right. We see that God states in *his word* that sexual contact must remain only between a man and his wife. And that pre-marital sex is a sin. I didn't say it, God wrote it in his word! God commands us to obey his rules. A *Truth* was revealed to you through God's word in *Hebrews 13:4 concerning sexual immortality.* Yes some of us have had pre-maritital sex thinking this was all right to do. These actions happened because of our *innocence, our ignorance, peer pressure, or low self esteem.* I tell you we were wrong, this immoral way was not the way God intended. So now that we know the truth it is time to sober up, clean out, clean up and evaluate your life. Take a personal inventory of yourself. Ask God to remove all doubt. To remove all our vain desires. And to give you strength not to yield to temptation, for we know yielding is *sin.* But also note that when or if you do fall into a sinful act. Don't lie there in the mud of the sin, and give up. Get yourself up. Standing firmly on your feet. Dust yourself off. And keep moving positively forward!

Then ask God to forgive you for your transgressions, promising that you will try again to walk closely in his will and his way. Trusting that he will guide you and keep you. You need to know that God can do all things, but you must start taking the *trash out* in your lives. *Hebrews 12:2,* Start removing all negative things or persons that are weighing you down and blocking you from seeing God, and your new life. Start reading your bible more, and start praying and talking to God more. Seek answers for your life through *prayer and meditation.* Join or reinstate to a church of your choice that is *Christ Centered.* Start making a life change. If you don't follow these simple instructions, then your lifestyle will not line up with *God's Will.* And you are living your life your way and not *God's Way.* Think about it, why would God send a good man to your immoral lifestyle to be destroyed? He wouldn't. You've got to live by God's rules ladies, if you want to be blessed.

Conclusion

Ask, Wait, Trust!

Finally, ask God for what you want, then trust God enough to wait on him to bless you with it, no matter how long it takes. Stay *faithful* to God's Word. Get busy in the Church Ministries, such as the Mission, Children's Church, Outreach Programs, or Sunday School, etc. There is always a need for people to work in the church. *Nehemiah 4:6*

Find a Ministry in which *you can work faithfully and joyfully.* Focus on the *First Love* of *your life, Jesus Christ,* and not on the fact that you are almost 40 and you still don't have a man! Women, if you want to find that good man, and men if you want to find that good woman, stay with God, trust Him, and he will send your love to you. Your life will change dramatically, If you just Trust God!

I know this for a fact. How do I know? Well, for two years I stopped dating because I was attracting the worst kind of men. So I prayed and asked God to find someone for me, since I was doing such a lousy job at it. I prayed and asked God to send someone who would love me for me. I prayed for someone to be a good husband, who would have a great Love for God, as I do. I wrote down my description list and stated it in my prayers. I also faithfully prayed for someone tall, cute, fun to be with and who had a sense of humor.

I continued working in the church and the community faithfully, trusting that God would hear and answer my prayers.

Praise Be to God! He sent me my love in the form of Reverend William A. Cunningham: My blessing, my husband of 25 years and counting. Bless the Lord! So you see ladies, you have to walk close to God, live within his will, and develop a relationship with him. Ask God to forgive you of your sins. Be faithful unto God. And He will bless you, and He will take care of you all the days of your life.

Repent, and put your life in God's hands, learning to totally trust God and make *Him the Sovereign Ruler of your life. When you have an active relationship with God, it is good to know that you can talk to God, and He will talk to you through His Word, through prayer, and He will speak to your mind through the Holy Ghost when you spend time in meditation and prayer to Him.* Study God's Word, store it in your heart, and pray often. Live, love, and proclaim Jesus! He will guide you if you let him. These are the few steps to meeting and marrying the love of your life. But, YOU MUST DO IT GOD'S WAY!

Thank you and God Bless!

References
Holy Bible King James Version
Where to Find It In The Bible-Author Ken Anderson
Nelson Publishers
The Ultimate A to Z Resource Book-Author Ken Anderson
Nelson Publishers
Webster's Dictionary

EXCERPTS FROM
THE AUTHOR

How To Be A Pastor Or Ministers Wife

(An encouraging word or two)
By Lillian Cunningham
World Wide MB Church

The truth is there is no set way to be a Ministers Wife. We are expected by God, the Pastor and the Church to be the *Help Mate* to our husbands. But, being your husband's helpmate does not mean you can tell him how to preach his sermon, nor can you tell him what to preach. The pulpit order is *Not* your concern. That's Gods business. The Associate Ministers Wives are to learn from the Pastors Wife by observance of how she conducts herself as she follows the instructions of her Pastor/Husband, as he follows Christ.

While at my monthly BM&E of Michigan (Biblical, Missionary, & Educational) State Ministers Wives and Widows meeting, one of the wives posed a series of questions to the ministers wives. Four questions were asked of us. This is a good exercise that could be discussed in your own meeting. How would your Minister Wives answer these questions? Here are some of the answers that were given that night.

- **<u>I want a Husband, Not a Pastor!</u>**
- Answer: He is my husband at home, but he is my pastor at church.

- **That was a Nice Sermon Honey, But..**
- Answer: But What? I'm sure he will look at you funny when you say but. Just make your point. The older more Traditional Pastors Wives of my group were not allowed to make comments on their husband's sermons, or pull them aside to discuss it. One lady from the old way stated it just wasn't done. They knew their place. They were not allowed to ask questions about it.
- **Who trains the Pastors Wife?**
- Answer: Some new Minister wives were blessed to have been trained by the former Pastors wife, while others learned by trial and error.
- **I am more than a Pastors/Ministers Wife! Who am I?**
- Answer; I am his lover, his friend, his confidant, his right hand, his wife, the mother of his children, and the one who prays daily to the Lord to give her husband strength to lead Gods people.

Last but not least stay encouraged. It's not easy being a Ministers Wife. But it's not hard either. Also know that everybody in the church does not love you! Yes, they love the Pastor, but not you. Strange isn't it? But true. Why? There are some women who want to be you. They are jealous because you are in the position they want to be in.

If they only knew that our job is not at all glamorous. Some of us like myself are not impressed whether or not being recognized when you walk into a banquet room on your husband's arm. Nor is it a big deal to some of us when we have to sit at the head tables. Or to be called *First Lady of the Church*. But if your church members want to acknowledge you as such, then let them. Just don't get the big head thinking you are better than everyone because you are a Pastor or Ministers wife. Stay Humble.

What is impressive to God is how you are up praying late at night for your husband as he walks the floor asking *Him* for *Spiritual* direction on how to lead the people of his church, or he's praying on how to help, and to see about this church members. God smiles when we ask Him to give our husbands an inspirational sermon to preach to the congregation. We Ministers wives do a lot of work in the church.

Sometimes it's us working side by side with our husbands giving out food to the needy, checking on the sick, working diligently in our various church ministries. Or driving our husband to the hospital at 2:00 am when he gets that call that a church member has died. We have to go when no one else will, we have to do when no one else will. How many times has our husbands volunteered us for a project when no one at the church would volunteer?

But even in all that we go through as Ministers Wives it is a blessing to be married to the Preacher! You know you are loved because of his deep love for Christ, his church, and for his family!

So celebrate ladies, God chose your husband out of love, and your husband chose you out of love. Thank You Lord for the many blessings! My Cup Runs Over!

I-Am-Ology

Spiritual and Mental Body Builders

1. I Am Positive
2. I Am Intelligent
3. I Am Concerned About Others
4. I Am An Ephesians Chapter 6 Warrior, Dressed for Spiritual Battle
5. I Am A Daily Bible Reader (Not Just On Sunday At Church)
6. I Am A Worshiper And A Disciple Of Jesus Christ
7. I Am On Time For Church.
   (If I can get to work on time, I can get to church on time)

I Am Positive!

A positive attitude will get you further along in life than a negative attitude will. The Holy Bible scripture states in Proverbs 23:7 that: Whatsoever a man thinks in his heart, so is he. This applies to the women also. So, if you're a consistent negative Nelly, than your life will reflect your negative behavior. And your family and friends will also see this less positive; nothing is ever right side of you as well. Some of your family or friends may choose not to be around you because your attitude is bringing them down. Here's a question, have you ever had someone say to you or to another person like you: don't bother asking him or her about the situation.

You know they don't have anything positive to say! All they do is complain? Now I ask you the reader, does this describe you? Are you the negative force in your life? Do you only see the glass half empty all the time? Could it be your negative thoughts and behavior has blocked you from some positive heavenly rewards? If this describes you, than you need a Mental and Spiritual transformation! First, your mental thinking must take a turn to the positive side. You ask how? You stated that you have been this way for as long as you can remember. And I say to you that you must step back and take a good long look at yourself and your present situation. Began to ask your self these questions: When did I start being so negative about everything? Where was I the most influenced by this negative attitude? Who or what helped to influence my negativity? How do I begin to change my life to think more positive? Those are the questions, now here are the answers. Lets evaluate.

1. Think back to the origin of when you began to think nothing was ever right. Write it down.
2. Think back to when suggestions or proposals were asked of you, and *your reply was that will never work, you can't do that, I don't see the potential, or the purpose.* Write it down.
3. Think back to my being in a meeting at work or at church when I eagerly raised my hand to give my suggestions or ideas and they were shot down or dismissed? Disappointed, never to offer my suggestions again. Write it down.
4. Or maybe this one describes you. My fears convinced me that my ideas and suggestions weren't good enough to be presented. So I gave into my fears and kept quiet. While getting angry with myself for being a coward. And then convincing myself that it wouldn't work anyway. Think back. And write it down.

After you have asked your self these questions and have written down your answers, take a good long look at your answers. Face them, see where your shortcomings are, see where the negative demon has had a hold on your life. Turn this negative into a positive. Rewrite each answer with a positive thought. Give yourself a chance. Stop thinking everything has to be no. Start saying yes, start thinking yes, quote the scripture: *I can do all things through Christ that strengthens me.* Pray and ask God to give you the strength and the courage that you need. Look for the good in any situation. Present your ideas; be bold and informative with your perspectives. Do your homework. Know what you're talking about. Think Positive. Move forward. Don't look back, because if you look back while moving forward you *will* run into a wall! Amen!

All right, we have addressed one side of why we are not positive. Let's get up close and personal. There is another reason as to why you have a less than positive attitude. Let's examine the younger you. After, all you didn't wake up one day and decided to live a negative life. So, the question is asked of you, who *were* the negative forces in your childhood, teen, young adult, or adult life? Who told you that you would never amount to anything? Or you're just like your daddy, the drunk? Who planted that negative seed in you, that you were worthless? Ugly? Not good for nothing? Who told you that you would never be successful in life? Stop the madness! Stop thinking about what was said to and about you long ago. Climb out of the rut of *no return.* Start thinking and living a positive, *yes I can life.* This transformation won't happen over night, it's a process. The next thing we must do in turning around our attitude is to *face them.* Don't be afraid to confront your past. Think about where the hurt began, if you keep concentrating you will see someone in your vision. Why, look, it's you! A younger version of you, the hurting you, the suppressed you, the one who has pushed the pain to the utter darkest part, way in the back of your mind, you. Grab hold to that hurting little person and take them by the hand, tell them that everything is fine now. Tell them that you love them. Tell them that we are moving forward into our positive future as adults. Free to do what we want. Free to excel as high as we want to go. Tell the *adolescent hurting you, that the new positive adult you* will not remain in the past afraid to take on new challenges. The new positive you, is leaving the bad things that happened to them, the shame and unhappiness behind, never to surface again. Once you truly believe in yourself the *old you* will began to fade as the *stronger positive you takes precedence over your life.* Learn to press forward in all your endeavors, trusting in God and believing that *He* will be *the positive force* in your life. In other words let the past go!

I Am Intelligent

Webster's Dictionary defines intelligence as having good understanding, and being quick to comprehend. Persons of intelligence display sound thought patterns in judgment, and can absorb and retain large quantities of knowledge in our memory like a sponge, a process that is achieved through our learning ability from infants to adulthood. As you know humans are born a blank slate as infants. But as we grow in our childhood, we are taught the fundamentals through a learning process. We start out learning to sound words such as, mama, daddy, hungry, milk, sleepy, etc. as the child grows so does the mobile skills, they learn to walk, run, sit, fall, and jump off everything, especially the furniture. Children are taught their ABC'S, how to count, they are taught their colors, and how to build things from their blocks. But nothing is more beautiful than when your toddler has figured out a puzzle or has accomplished a goal, like climbing to the stop of the stairs by themselves and coming down by themselves. The look of: *I did it, by myself* is splashed all over their little faces. And the look of panic is on ours as we rush to catch them in case they decide to jump from the top stairs. Our children are not afraid, and they love a challenge. The parent teaches fear. When we are afraid to let our children learn by trying new things we hinder them. No, I don't mean letting the child walk out into traffic, or pulling on electric plugs. I'm saying their little minds are curious, and they have a lot of questions. At two years old the parent is bombarded with the *why* questions, because they want to know. The child is absorbing what they have learned. Yes, teach your child that they cannot touch a hot stove, teach them that they cannot play with electric appliances, tell them the truth, that it will hurt them if you touch it.

If they ask a question, answer them. Don't tell them to shut up and go sit down, tell them why. And after you have answered the little ones question to the best of your ability, then you can tell them, I answered your question, or I don't know why to that question. So let's do something else, go into your room and color, or go watch TV, and we will ask daddy or mommy when they get home. That answer usually works for a short while, giving you a break. I'm not a child psychologist; I don't have any type of degree in that area. But I do know what works in my house with my three-year-old grandson. As I was saying while we are growing our desire to learn grows along with us. Reading and writing is now exciting and we have a desire to learn more. We are absorbing as much knowledge possible. A great many of us have achieved our scholastic goals in life and have moved further up the academic and society ladder. While at the same time we have a great many who have fallen short of going to school, dropped out, family circumstances got in the way, or their flamed desire for higher education was snuffed out by someone or something that told them they would never make it. So they just stopped pursuing their dreams, stopped moving forward. Just at a standstill. Existing in the world, with no plans for the future, with no goals to pursue. Going no-where by express! But wait, I'm here to tell you that it's not too late to pursue your dreams. It's never too late to begin again. Only when you're *dead,* then it's too late. So what if you're age 30 or older going back to school. You are *alive!* Pursue your dreams! Remember that scripture I told you to quote? *Philippians 4:13: I can do all things through Christ that strengthens me.* Do you believe it? Add this quote to your daily routine. Live by it.

Believe it. Believe that through Jesus Christ you can do anything! Go back to school and get your GED or your college degree that you didn't get before because of whatever reason, its time to think about yourself. You're a smart person, use your brain for more than playing video games or sending senseless *selfies* from your phone to Face Book, Twitter, Photo Grid, etc. I tell you that you are a smart person, because God made you in his image. Read *Genesis 1:26-31*. It's the very first book in the bible for some of you who don't know. (Just a bible tip not being funny.) You will see after you read the passage in Genesis, that God gave you spiritual, mental, and physical power. We just have to tap into ourselves and use what we were given. Knowledge is your power acquired through learning. We know that the definition of knowledge is an accumulation of learned facts that we have set to memory. In order to obtain knowledge we must read books, and informative articles. Knowledge is food for the brain. Feed it! Learn what is needed for you to live and work in today's society. Get as much education as you can. Absorb as much knowledge as you can without sending your brain into overload. Now, I don't want you to have only a knowledgeable character, but God wants you to be wise also. So to obtain this attribute you must have an *active relationship* with *God.* Why? Because wisdom comes from God, read *James 1:5.* Here God says to *ask for Wisdom and he will give it liberally.*

We must put the negative ideas about ourselves aside. We must stop thinking negative. We must stop mutilating ourselves with negativity. How am I doing that? You ask. Well when you put your own self down, you are mutilating your self-esteem. When you think you are less beautiful, less motivating, not as worthy as anyone else, you have just shot yourself in the head. Take a good long look in the mirror at yourself. Ask yourself, why am I here? Why did God wake me this morning? What is my contribution to the world? Here are some of the answers. You are alive for a reason. Your task is to make an impact on the world, if not the world, maybe in your neighborhood, your school, church, synagogue, or your family. It doesn't matter whether the impact is large or small. Make one anyway. *Be the best you can be, a corny line, but a very true one.* Show the world that you are an intelligent, God fearing individual who can accomplish any goal that is set before them. Show society that you can live as a law-abiding citizen who has a passion for God and country. Show them the positive you. Not the one that society thinks of you. As an unintelligent, jail bound minority, who will never be anything but someone who depends only on the State Welfare System looking for handouts. You are more that. *You must become the positive factor in your life!* Now repeat after me: I AM A BEAUTIFUL, AND WISE PERSON OF INTELLUCTIAL POTENTIAL! Never, let a person or a situation be your dream killer! Stay Positive!

I Am An Ephesians 6: 13 Warrior

Dressed for Battle
Ephesians 6:13-18

The best way to talk about this page is to just let you read it for yourselves.

God says:

- To put on the whole armor of God, that you may be able to withstand in the evil day, and having done all stand.
- Stand therefore having girded your waist with truth
- Having put on the breastplate of righteousness
- And having shod your feet with the preparation of the gospel of peace
- Above all, taking the shield of faith with which you will be able to quench all the fiery darts of the wicked one
- And take the helmet of salvation,

- And the sword of the Spirit, which is the word of God.
- Praying always with all prayer and supplication in the Spirit, being watchful to this end with all perseverance and supplication for all the saints

Are you dress for battle? Are you wearing all your armor? Half a suit won't do. You must be fully dressed and ready to fight the evil one. Come on get dressed!

I Am Concerned About Others

We are our brother's keepers, whether we like it or not. We are to be concerned about others, not just ourselves. The bible states in *Philippians 2: 3-4: Let nothing be done in vain glory. But in lowliness of mind, let each esteem others better than themselves. Look not every man on his own things, but every man also on the things of others. Let this mind be in you, which is in Christ Jesus.*

God has set the standard for us. Be concerned for your fellow man. Love one another also. God commands in *John 13: 34: A new commandment that I give you, that you love one another as I have loved you, that you also love one another.* Listed here are other scriptures on loving one another, please also read: *Suggested scriptures: John 15:17, John 15: 12, I John 4:11, Roman 13:8, and I John 3:11.*

There are at least twenty verses on loving others, take time to read the scriptures and apply one or more of them to your life. Like the song says, *Put A Little Love In Your Heart!* Try it, you'll feel better!

I Am A Worshiper, Daily Bible Reader, And A True Follower of Christ!

When you decide give your life to God, and choose to follow the teachings of the Gospel of Jesus Christ, you have taken the biggest step ever, and your life will begin to change for the better. No, you will not stop having problems, and your trials and tribulations will not go away. In fact your problems will increase, once you give God your life, because Satan is angry that you chose God over him. But do not get dismayed for the difference between you, the saved-confessed Christian and the non-believer is that you have a savior named Jesus, God's only son to tell your problems to and to resolve them. Yes, problems bog down the best of Christian Saints, but the key is that the true believers of God refuse to stay bogged down. We simply call on our God to have mercy, and to help us. And he does just that. God will give us peace in the middle of our storms in life. God has promised us that he is with us always, and he will never leave us. It is our *Faith* in him that keeps us afloat. It is our *faith* in God that helps us to cry for a minuet in our circumstances, and then to remember that God will take care of our problems. Our Faith reminds us to stop crying over our burdens and to start praising God in the middle of our circumstances. God is true to his word *HE* always brings us out. It is only because of our faith in God that we can laugh at our negative situations. We believe that *HE* is real and that *HE* is true to his word. The true believer stands firmly on the word of God. We worship *HIM* not just for what he has done. Such as create the world, formed man from the dust of the earth and breathed his breath into us, making man living souls. We thank God for that. We thank and worship *God for His "So" love* (St. John 3:16 King James Version) for the world by sending *His son Jesus* to *redeem and save us*, and *His Holy Spirit to Comfort us.* We praise, worship and thank God for all he has done, and what *HE* continues to do in our lives! *Thank You Lord.* We *also worship God for who he is. The one True God, King of Kings, and Lord of Lords. Lilly Of The Valley,* the Bright and Morning Star. *My provider, my Heavenly Father, my true friend, He's my everything.* I believe the bible to be the *true living word of God.* I believe all sixty-six books. And I am a disciple, which means follower of the *Gospel Of Jesus Christ.*

Listen people I'm not perfect by any means, I mess up, and I fall short as any human would. But the reward is that when I have realized that I have fallen from Gods Grace and have let sin separate me from God. I pick myself up and repent of my ways, asking humbly for Gods forgiveness and strength to do better and to be stronger to not yield so quickly to the world's temptations. When we come to God with a humble heart and sincerity in our prayers, God will hear and answer us because he sees our sincerity and he forgives us, taking us back into *His* family. I may not be as outstanding as some of you in memorizing biblical scriptures, but one thing I do know definitely, that God lives in me and I am one of His children. My relationship is alive and well. I know Jesus for myself. I worship God in Spirit and in Truth! Finally, in those blessed preached words of my husband Pastor Cunningham, I remember him telling his associate ministers, when you talking about the goodness of Jesus Christ, don't forget to go to the cross. Well, I'm not a minister but…*One Friday, out on a hill called Calvary, Jesus was nailed to a rugged cross, He endured the torture of a terrible death because he loved mankind. And only a sinless Jesus could redeem us back to God. Jesus died, but he didn't stay dead, and, early Sunday morning, Jesus got up, with All Power in His hands, All Power in Heaven and in Earth. Halleluiah! And because He rose, I can rise above my circumstances. Because He rose I don't have to stay down in a stagnant situation, I too can rise above it. He gave us a chance. He gave our souls a permanent heavenly home. That's why I praise Him, that's why I love Him, that's why I cherish and read his word, because He first loved me! He left his home in Glory to save someone like me, a speck of dust, a bubble on the face of the water, a temporary being. Jesus came down from heaven for me. Thank You Lord God!* Try Jesus for yourself, I guarantee your life will never be the same again! *Oh, Come let us worship the Lord in the*

beauty of Holiness. Give Him the Honor, give Him the Praise, come,
let us worship the Lord, and let's give Him the Praise!

I Am On Time For Church

(If I can get to work on time, I can get to church on time)

Last but not least, try getting to service on time. If you come
to morning Sunday School, than you will already be on time for
church. Just a thought you might want to consider in the future.
When you're late it is so annoying to everybody, to the ushers who
have to try to seat you during the middle of service. It's annoying to
the people in the row that the ushers are trying to seat you in. What
make you think I want to move down from my isle seat to give it to
you? I sat there for a reason. And it really burns my cookies when
you try step over me, smashing my feet, snagging my hosiery with
your shoe as you try to get to an empty seat in the middle of the row.
It's bad enough that you didn't wait until I got up to let you in, and
you decided to barrel through, now I'm leaning back to keep your
rear-end, your purse, and his hat and coat out of my face as you two
try to pass. Then I'm hearing empty apologies from you: *excuse me,*
sorry, oops, sorry about your foot. Yeah, whatever, just hurry up and
sit down! I'm thinking. Sometimes I wish I had a great big stick
pin so I could jab them in the fanny as they crawl over me to get to
their seat. Ouch! I know that's not the Christian way to think about
your fellow sisters or brothers, but you must admit it was a funny
thought. So, late people try to change your ways, work at being on-
time people. Your day will go a lot smoother with less frustration
and fuss. I always say if you can get to work on time to a company
that cares nothing about you, and only care that you do your job
to keep *their* production going, and to help *their* company make
money. You can be on time to church for God, the one who gave
you life, who loves you, shelters you, protects and keeps you. God

wakes you every morning with a finger of love to go to that job he gave you. And rocks you to sleep at night with angels watching over you and your family. Surely you could show gratitude by getting to church on time to worship, adore and praise him. Please read *Psalms 100*. It instructs you on how to enter into Gods house with praise and worship. You need to know what is primary in your life. What do you think it is? Here's a hint: God says everything in the world and in heaven belongs to him. Including your job. Make God first, keep his commandments and he will open the windows of heaven and pour out blessings you won't have room to receive. *Malachi 3:10*

Put God first, Family second, than you. Make time for God, He made time to come down from heaven to save you.

Amen.

My Feelings Paper

My Sister Gracie Mae Johnson

My sister Gracie died. May 24, 2014 at 7:25 am in St. John Hospital of Grosse Pointe Michigan. She died on my first cousin Theressa's birthday. A celebration of a life for one still here, and a home going celebration for one gone on to glory. My sister died. Even after the funeral I am at a stand still. Oh, I thank God for my life, and I thank *Him* for the time spent with my sister. We were twenty-one years apart. She was eighty-three and I am sixty-two. But, I had gotten use to her being around. Funny how we think our love ones will live forever. Still, I miss her and I feel alone. Mommy and Daddy are gone, and now Gracie Mae. I am the only one left of my original family. No other siblings. Just me. Oh Lord how long does this grieving process take? When will the heartache and the pain subside? When will the hurting end? My sister Gracie Mae died! God please help me to break these grieving chains. Break the chains of grief! Break the chains of heartache! I have to face reality my sister died and she is gone. Some of me died with her. But I refuse to stay in this grief stricken rut. I pray to God for help and I will strive to climb out of this black hole. One heartache, and one tear at a time, Until the pain of my loss fades to a numbness and then the numbness fades to one small lump of hurt that I will lock away in my heart. I will think of the happy times I shared with my sister, such as setting the dining room table as a child for holiday dinners with her prized possession of bone china dinnerware, crystal goblets and sterling silver flatware. *How beautiful the table looks, she would say to me.* I'm thinking of how my sister taught me to make her famous yeast milk-less rolls. Mississippi bread as she called it. So many thoughts are going through my mind now, Her voice, her laughter, the way she shouted at church as she professed her love for Jesus Christ, I even miss her anger. So many stories I could tell about the trouble I got into with the two older brothers of her four sons, they were like the brothers I never had. And to her two younger sons and her only daughter, I was their babysitter. Five children my sister had, Leon jr. Gordon, Billy Samuel, Ellis David and Carol Ann. And then there was me, *Auntie Bae-Bae.* A name and a title none of her kids respected until they got grown. Hilarious. I was ten years old when I came to live with them after our mother died, Gracie, and mines. Her children were younger also. So being called aunt anything was out of the question for them. And at ten years old who wants to be called auntie, sounds ancient. I remember my sister always had a smile for you, and would help anyone that needed it. I thank God that I can think on those precious happy memories that my sister and I shared. My sister may be gone from this earth, but she was a devout Christian and she told everyone she met how she loved God. My sister Gracie Mae died, but she now lives in heaven with God.

May I live a life so close to God as she did, so that one day I can see her smiling face again.

My very wise daughter Danielle told me to sit down and write out my emotions. She said I would feel better and she was right. I love my daughter's wisdom. She's my gift from God, and I thank *Him* for her. I feel better since I wrote this piece last June 2014. I miss and love you, Gracie Mae. My big sister, my heart, rest in peace until we meet again in eternity.

Love,
Your little Sister, Lillian.

Thank you Lord God for giving me peace, and for giving my family peace in our time of bereavement. Thank you for wiping away the tears, and mending the broken hearts. Thank you Lord God for helping me to think on the good memories of my sister. Thank you Lord God for your comfort! It is true that God will keep you in perfect peace, if you keep your mind on him. He is a heart fixer! Bless that wonderful name of Jesus!

CPSIA information can be obtained
at www.ICGtesting.com
Printed in the USA
FFOW04n2219310715
15634FF